THE ART OF PEACE

T0112930

MORIHEI UESHIBA

THE ART
OF PEACE

Teachings of the Founder
of Aikido

Compiled & translated by
JOHN STEVENS

SHAMBHALA
Boulder
1992

Shambhala Publications, Inc.
2129 13th Street
Boulder, Colorado 80302
www.shambhala.com

34 33 32 31 30 29 28 27 26

Printed in Canada
Shambhala Publications makes every effort to print
on acid-free, recycled paper.
Shambhala Publications is distributed worldwide by
Penguin Random House, Inc., and its subsidiaries.

See page 126 for Library of Congress
Cataloging-in-Publication data.

INTRODUCTION

Morihei Ueshiba (1883–1969) was history's greatest martial artist. Even as an old man of eighty, Morihei could disarm any foe, down any number of attackers, and pin an opponent with a single finger. Although invincible as a warrior, Morihei was above all a man of peace who detested fighting, war, and any kind of violence. His way was Aikido, which can be translated as "The Art of Peace."

The Art of Peace is an ideal, but it developed in real life on many fronts. Morihei in his youth served as an infantryman in the Russo-Japanese War, later battled pirates and bandits during an adventure in Mongolia, and then, after mastering a number of martial arts, served as an instructor at Japan's elite military academies. Throughout his life, however, Morihei was sorely troubled by the contention and strife that plagued his world: his father's battles with corrupt politicians and their hired goons, the devastation of war, and the brutality of his country's military leaders.

Morihei was on a spiritual quest and was transformed by three visions. The first occurred in 1925, when Morihei was forty-two years old. After defeating a high-ranking swordsman by avoiding all his cuts and thrusts (Morihei was unarmed), Morihei went into his garden. "Suddenly the earth trembled. Golden vapor welled up from the ground and engulfed me. I felt transformed into a golden image, and my body seemed as light as a feather. All at once I understood the nature of creation: the Way of a Warrior is to manifest Divine

Love, a spirit that embraces and nurtures all things. Tears of gratitude and joy streamed down my cheeks. I saw the entire earth as my home, and the sun, moon, and stars as my intimate friends. All attachment to material things vanished."

The second vision took place in December of 1940. "Around two o'clock in the morning as I was performing ritual purification, I suddenly forgot every martial art technique I had ever learned. All of the techniques handed down from my teachers appeared completely anew. Now they were vehicles for the cultivation of life, knowledge, virtue, and good sense, not devices to throw and pin people."

The third vision was in 1942, during the worst of the fighting of World War II and in one of the darkest periods of human history. Morihei had a vision of the Great Spirit of Peace, a path that could lead to the elimination of all strife and the reconciliation of humankind. "The Way of the Warrior has been misunderstood as a means to kill and destroy others. Those who seek competition are making a grave mistake. To smash, injure, or destroy is the worst sin a human being can commit. The real Way of a Warrior is to prevent slaughter—it is the Art of Peace, the power of love." Morihei secluded himself in the country and devoted every minute of his life thereafter to refining and spreading Aikido, the Art of Peace.

Unlike the authors of old-time warrior classics such as *The Art of War* and *The Book of Five Rings*, which accept the inevitability of war and emphasize cunning strategy as a means to victory, Morihei understood that continued fighting—with others, with ourselves, and with the environment—will ruin the earth. "The world will continue to change dramatically, but fighting and war can destroy us utterly. What we need now are techniques of harmony, not those of contention. The Art of Peace is required, not the Art of War." Morihei taught the Art of Peace as a creative mind-body discipline, as a practical means of handling aggression, and as a way of life that fosters fearlessness, wisdom, love, and friendship. He interpreted the Art of Peace in the broadest possible sense and believed that its principles of reconciliation, harmony, cooperation, and empathy could be applied bravely to all the challenges we face in life—in personal relationships, as we interact with society, at work and in business, when dealing with nature. Everyone can be a warrior for peace.

Although Aikido originated with Morihei in Japan, it was intended to be a gift for all humankind. Some have chosen, or will select in the future, Aikido as their own particular Way, practicing it on the mats and applying it to their daily lives. Many more have been and will be, I hope, inspired by the universal message of the Art of Peace and its implications for our world.

> The divine beauty
> Of heaven and earth!
> All creation,
> Members of
> One family.

The quotations in this book have been compiled from Morihei's collected talks, poems, and calligraphy, and from oral tradition.

The term *ki* (*ch'i* in Chinese) occurs in a few places; this refers to the subtle energy that propels the universe, the vitality that pervades creation and holds things together.

THE ART OF PEACE

THE ART OF PEACE begins with you. Work on yourself and your appointed task in the Art of Peace. Everyone has a spirit that can be refined, a body that can be trained in some manner, a suitable path to follow. You are here for no other purpose than to realize your inner divinity and manifest your innate enlightenment. Foster peace in your own life and then apply the Art to all that you encounter.

ONE does not need buildings, money, power, or status to practice the Art of Peace. Heaven is right where you are standing, and that is the place to train.

ALL THINGS, material and spiritual, originate from one source and are related as if they were one family. The past, present, and future are all contained in the life force. The universe emerged and developed from one source, and we evolved through the optimal process of unification and harmonization.

THE ART OF PEACE is medicine for a sick world. There is evil and disorder in the world because people have forgotten that all things emanate from one source. Return to that source and leave behind all self-centered thoughts, petty desires, and anger. Those who are possessed by nothing possess everything.

IF you have not
Linked yourself
To true emptiness,
You will never understand
The Art of Peace.

THE ART OF PEACE functions everywhere on earth, in realms ranging from the vastness of space down to the tiniest plants and animals. The life force is all-pervasive and its strength boundless. The Art of Peace allows us to perceive and tap into that tremendous reserve of universal energy.

EIGHT forces sustain creation:
Movement and stillness,
Solidification and fluidity,
Extension and contraction,
Unification and division.

LIFE is growth. If we stop growing, technically and spiritually, we are as good as dead. The Art of Peace is a celebration of the bonding of heaven, earth, and humankind. It is all that is true, good, and beautiful.

Now and again, it is necessary to se-
clude yourself among deep mountains
and hidden valleys to restore your link to
the source of life. Breathe in and let
yourself soar to the ends of the universe;
breathe out and bring the cosmos back
inside. Next, breathe up all the fecundity
and vibrancy of the earth. Finally, blend
the breath of heaven and the breath of
earth with that of your own, becoming
the Breath of Life itself.

ALL the principles of heaven and earth are living inside you. Life itself is the truth, and this will never change. Everything in heaven and earth breathes. Breath is the thread that ties creation together. When the myriad variations in the universal breath can be sensed, the individual techniques of the Art of Peace are born.

CONSIDER the ebb and flow of the tide. When waves come to strike the shore, they crest and fall, creating a sound. Your breath should follow the same pattern, absorbing the entire universe in your belly with each inhalation. Know that we all have access to four treasures: the energy of the sun and moon, the breath of heaven, the breath of earth, and the ebb and flow of the tide.

THOSE who practice the Art of Peace must protect the domain of Mother Nature, the divine reflection of creation, and keep it lovely and fresh. Warriorship gives birth to natural beauty. The subtle techniques of a warrior arise as naturally as the appearance of spring, summer, autumn, and winter. Warriorship is none other than the vitality that sustains all life.

WHEN life is victorious, there is birth; when it is thwarted, there is death. A warrior is always engaged in a life-and-death struggle for Peace.

CONTEMPLATE the workings of this world, listen to the words of the wise, and take all that is good as your own. With this as your base, open your own door to truth. Do not overlook the truth that is right before you. Study how water flows in a valley stream, smoothly and freely between the rocks. Also learn from holy books and wise people. Everything—even mountains, rivers, plants, and trees—should be your teacher.

CREATE each day anew by clothing yourself with heaven and earth, bathing yourself with wisdom and love, and placing yourself in the heart of Mother Nature.

Do not fail
To learn from
The pure voice of an
Ever-flowing mountain stream
Splashing over the rocks.

PEACE originates with the flow of things—its heart is like the movement of the wind and waves. The Way is like the veins that circulate blood through our bodies, following the natural flow of the life force. If you are separated in the slightest from that divine essence, you are far off the path.

YOUR heart is full of fertile seeds, waiting to sprout. Just as a lotus flower springs from the mire to bloom splendidly, the interaction of the cosmic breath causes the flower of the spirit to bloom and bear fruit in this world.

STUDY the teachings of the pine tree, the bamboo, and the plum blossom. The pine is evergreen, firmly rooted, and venerable. The bamboo is strong, resilient, unbreakable. The plum blossom is hardy, fragrant, and elegant.

ALWAYS keep your mind as bright and clear as the vast sky, the great ocean, and the highest peak, empty of all thoughts. Always keep your body filled with light and heat. Fill yourself with the power of wisdom and enlightenment.

As soon as you concern yourself with the "good" and "bad" of your fellows, you create an opening in your heart for maliciousness to enter. Testing, competing with, and criticizing others weaken and defeat you.

THE penetrating brilliance of swords
Wielded by followers of the Way
Strikes at the evil enemy
Lurking deep within
Their own souls and bodies.

THE ART OF PEACE is not easy. It is a fight to the finish, the slaying of evil desires and all falsehood within. On occasion the Voice of Peace resounds like thunder, jolting human beings out of their stupor.

CRYSTAL clear,
Sharp and bright,
The sacred sword
Allows no opening
For evil to roost.

To practice properly the Art of Peace,
you must:

Calm the spirit and return to the
source.

Cleanse the body and spirit by removing
all malice, selfishness, and desire.

Be ever-grateful for the gifts received
from the universe, your family,
Mother Nature, and your fellow
human beings.

THE ART OF PEACE is based on Four Great Virtues: Bravery, Wisdom, Love, and Friendship, symbolized by Fire, Heaven, Earth, and Water.

THE essence of the Art of Peace is to cleanse yourself of maliciousness, to get in tune with your environment, and to clear your path of all obstacles and barriers.

THE only cure for materialism is the cleansing of the six senses (eyes, ears, nose, tongue, body, and mind). If the senses are clogged, one's perception is stifled. The more it is stifled, the more contaminated the senses become. This creates disorder in the world, and that is the greatest evil of all. Polish the heart, free the six senses and let them function without obstruction, and your entire body and soul will glow.

ALL life is a manifestation of the spirit, the manifestation of love. And the Art of Peace is the purest form of that principle. A warrior is charged with bringing a halt to all contention and strife. Universal love functions in many forms; each manifestation should be allowed free expression. The Art of Peace is true democracy.

EACH and every master, regardless of the era or place, heard the call and attained harmony with heaven and earth. There are many paths leading to the top of Mount Fuji, but there is only one summit—love.

LOYALTY and devotion lead to bravery. Bravery leads to the spirit of self-sacrifice. The spirit of self-sacrifice creates trust in the power of love.

ECONOMY is the basis of society. When the economy is stable, society develops. The ideal economy combines the spiritual and material, and the best commodities to trade in are sincerity and love.

THE ART OF PEACE does not rely on weapons or brute force to succeed; instead we put ourselves in tune with the universe, maintain peace in our own realms, nurture life, and prevent death and destruction. The true meaning of the term *samurai* is one who serves and adheres to the power of love.

FOSTER and polish
The warrior spirit
While serving in the world;
Illuminate the Path
According to your inner light.

THE PATH OF PEACE is exceedingly vast, reflecting the grand design of the hidden and manifest worlds. A warrior is a living shrine of the divine, one who serves that grand purpose.

Your mind should be in harmony with the functioning of the universe; your body should be in tune with the movement of the universe; body and mind should be bound as one, unified with the activity of the universe.

EVEN though our path is completely different from the warrior arts of the past, it is not necessary to abandon totally the old ways. Absorb venerable traditions into this new Art by clothing them with fresh garments, and build on the classic styles to create better forms.

DAILY training in the Art of Peace allows your inner divinity to shine brighter and brighter. Do not concern yourself with the right and wrong of others. Do not be calculating or act unnaturally. Keep your mind set on the Art of Peace, and do not criticize other teachers or traditions. The Art of Peace never restrains, restricts, or shackles anything. It embraces all and purifies everything.

PRACTICE the Art of Peace sincerely, and evil thoughts and deeds will naturally disappear. The only desire that should remain is the thirst for more and more training in the Way.

THOSE who are enlightened never stop forging themselves. The realizations of such masters cannot be expressed well in words or by theories. The most perfect actions echo the patterns found in nature.

DAY after day
Train your heart out,
Refining your technique:
Use the One to strike the Many!
That is the discipline of a Warrior.

THE Way of a Warrior
Cannot be encompassed
By words or in letters:
Grasp the essence
And move on toward realization!

THE purpose of training is to tighten up the slack, toughen the body, and polish the spirit.

IRON is full of impurities that weaken it; through forging, it becomes steel and is transformed into a razor-sharp sword. Human beings develop in the same fashion.

FROM ancient times,
Deep learning and valor
Have been the two pillars of the Path:
Through the virtue of training,
Enlighten both body and soul.

INSTRUCTORS can impart only a fraction of the teaching. It is through your own devoted practice that the mysteries of the Art of Peace are brought to life.

THE Way of a Warrior is based on humanity, love, and sincerity; the heart of martial valor is true bravery, wisdom, love, and friendship. Emphasis on the physical aspects of warriorship is futile, for the power of the body is always limited.

A true warrior is always armed with the three things: the radiant sword of pacification; the mirror of bravery, wisdom, and friendship; and the precious jewel of enlightenment.

THE heart of a human being is no different from the soul of heaven and earth. In your practice always keep in your thoughts the interaction of heaven and earth, water and fire, *yin* and *yang*.

THE ART OF PEACE is the principle of nonresistance. Because it is nonresistant, it is victorious from the beginning. Those with evil intentions or contentious thoughts are instantly vanquished. The Art of Peace is invincible because it contends with nothing.

THERE are no contests in the Art of Peace. A true warrior is invincible because he or she contests with nothing. *Defeat* means to defeat the mind of contention that we harbor within.

To injure an opponent is to injure yourself. To control aggression without in-
flicting injury is the Art of Peace.

THE totally awakened warrior can freely utilize all elements contained in heaven and earth. The true warrior learns how to correctly perceive the activity of the universe and how to transform martial techniques into vehicles of purity, goodness, and beauty. A warrior's mind and body must be permeated with enlightened wisdom and deep calm.

ALWAYS practice the Art of Peace in a vibrant and joyful manner.

It is necessary to develop a strategy that utilizes all the physical conditions and elements that are directly at hand. The best strategy relies upon an unlimited set of responses.

A good stance and posture reflect a proper state of mind.

THE key to good technique is to keep your hands, feet, and hips straight and centered. If you are centered, you can move freely. The physical center is your belly; if your mind is set there as well, you are assured of victory in any endeavor.

MOVE like a beam of light:
Fly like lightning,
Strike like thunder,
Whirl in circles around
A stable center.

TECHNIQUES employ four qualities that reflect the nature of our world. Depending on the circumstance, you should be: hard as a diamond, flexible as a willow, smooth-flowing like water, or as empty as space.

IF your opponent strikes with fire, counter with water, becoming completely fluid and free-flowing. Water, by its nature, never collides with or breaks against anything. On the contrary, it swallows up any attack harmlessly.

FUNCTIONING harmoniously together, right and left give birth to all techniques. The left hand takes hold of life and death; the right hand controls it. The four limbs of the body are the four pillars of heaven, and manifest the eight directions, *yin* and *yang,* outer and inner.

MANIFEST *yang*
In your right hand,
Balance it with
The *yin* of your left,
And guide your partner.

THE techniques of the Art of Peace are neither fast nor slow, nor are they inside or outside. They transcend time and space.

SPRING forth from the Great Earth;
Billow like Great Waves;
Stand like a tree, sit like a rock;
Use the One to strike All.
Learn and forget!

WHEN an opponent comes forward, move in and greet him; if he wants to pull back, send him on his way.

THE body should be triangular, the mind circular. The triangle represents the generation of energy and is the most stable physical posture. The circle symbolizes serenity and perfection, the source of unlimited techniques. The square stands for solidity, the basis of applied control.

ALWAYS try to be in communion with heaven and earth; then the world will appear in its true light. Self-conceit will vanish, and you can blend with any attack.

IF your heart is large enough to envelop your adversaries, you can see right through them and avoid their attacks. And once you envelop them, you will be able to guide them along a path indicated to you by heaven and earth.

FREE of weakness,
No-mindedly ignore
The sharp attacks
Of your enemies:
Step in and act!

Do not look upon this world with fear and loathing. Bravely face whatever the gods offer.

EACH day of human life contains joy and anger, pain and pleasure, darkness and light, growth and decay. Each moment is etched with nature's grand design—do not try to deny or oppose the cosmic order of things.

PROTECTORS of this world
And guardians of the Ways
Of gods and buddhas,
The techniques of Peace
Enable us to meet every challenge.

LIFE itself is always a trial. In training, you must test and polish yourself in order to face the great challenges of life. Transcend the realm of life and death, and then you will be able to make your way calmly and safely through any crisis that confronts you.

BE grateful even for hardship, setbacks, and bad people. Dealing with such obstacles is an essential part of training in the Art of Peace.

FAILURE is the key to success;
Each mistake teaches us something.

IN extreme situations, the entire universe becomes our foe; at such critical times, unity of mind and technique is essential—do not let your heart waver!

AT the instant
A warrior
Confronts a foe,
All things
Come into focus.

EVEN when called out
By a single foe,
Remain on guard,
For you are always surrounded
By a host of enemies.

THE ART OF PEACE is to fulfill that which is lacking.

ONE should be prepared to receive ninety-nine percent of an enemy's attack and stare death right in the face in order to illumine the Path.

IN our techniques we enter completely
into, blend totally with, and control
firmly an attack. Strength resides where
one's *ki* is concentrated and stable; con-
fusion and maliciousness arise when *ki*
stagnates.

THERE are two types of *ki*: ordinary *ki* and true *ki*. Ordinary *ki* is coarse and heavy; true *ki* is light and versatile. In order to perform well, you have to liberate yourself from ordinary *ki* and permeate your organs with true *ki*. That is the basis of powerful technique.

In the Art of Peace we never attack. An attack is proof that one is out of control. Never run away from any kind of challenge, but do not try to suppress or control an opponent unnaturally. Let attackers come any way they like and then blend with them. Never chase after opponents. Redirect each attack and get firmly behind it.

SEEING me before him,
The enemy attacks,
But by that time
I am already standing
Safely behind him.

WHEN attacked, unify the upper, middle, and lower parts of your body. Enter, turn, and blend with your opponent, front and back, right and left.

YOUR spirit is the true shield.

OPPONENTS confront us continually, but actually there is no opponent there. Enter deeply into an attack and neutralize it as you draw that misdirected force into your own sphere.

Do not stare into the eyes of your opponent: he may mesmerize you. Do not fix your gaze on his sword: he may intimidate you. Do not focus on your opponent at all: he may absorb your energy. The essence of training is to bring your opponent completely into your sphere. Then you can stand just where you like.

EVEN the most powerful human being has a limited sphere of strength. Draw him outside of that sphere and into your own, and his strength will dissipate.

LEFT and right,
Avoid all
Cuts and parries.
Seize your opponents' minds
And scatter them all!

THE real Art of Peace is not to sacrifice a single one of your warriors to defeat an enemy. Vanquish your foes by always keeping yourself in a safe and unassailable position; then no one will suffer any losses. The Way of a Warrior, the Art of Politics, is to stop trouble before it starts. It consists in defeating your adversaries spiritually by making them realize the folly of their actions. The Way of a Warrior is to establish harmony.

MASTER the divine techniques
Of the Art of Peace,
And no enemy
Will dare to
Challenge you.

IN your training, do not be in a hurry, for it takes a minimum of ten years to master the basics and advance to the first rung. Never think of yourself as an all-knowing, perfected master; you must continue to train daily with your friends and students and progress together in the Art of Peace.

PROGRESS comes
To those who
Train and train;
Reliance on secret techniques
Will get you nowhere.

FIDDLING with this
And that technique
Is of no avail.
Simply act decisively
Without reserve!

IF you perceive the true form of heaven and earth, you will be enlightened to your own true form. If you are enlightened about a certain principle, you can put it into practice. After each practical application, reflect on your efforts. Progress continually like this.

THE ART OF PEACE can be summed up like this: *True victory is self-victory; let that day arrive quickly!* "True victory" means unflinching courage; "self-victory" symbolizes unflagging effort; and "let that day arrive quickly" represents the glorious moment of triumph in the here and now.

CAST off limiting thoughts and return to true emptiness. Stand in the midst of the Great Void. This is the secret of the Way of a Warrior.

To truly implement the Art of Peace, you must be able to sport freely in the manifest, hidden, and divine realms.

IF you comprehend
The Art of Peace,
This difficult path,
Just as it is,
Envelops the circle of heaven.

THE techniques of the Way of Peace change constantly; every encounter is unique, and the appropriate response should emerge naturally. Today's techniques will be different tomorrow. Do not get caught up with the form and appearance of a challenge. The Art of Peace has no form—it is the study of the spirit.

ULTIMATELY, you must forget about technique. The further you progress, the fewer teachings there are. The Great Path is really No Path.

THE ART OF PEACE that I practice has room for each of the world's eight million gods, and I cooperate with them all. The God of Peace is very great and enjoins all that is divine and enlightened in every land.

THE ART OF PEACE is a form of prayer that generates light and heat. Forget about your little self, detach yourself from objects, and you will radiate light and warmth. Light is wisdom; warmth is compassion.

CONSTRUCTION of shrine and temple buildings is not enough. Establish yourself as a living buddha image. We all should be transformed into goddesses of compassion or victorious buddhas.

Rely on Peace
To activate your
Manifold powers;
Pacify your environment
And create a beautiful world.

THE DIVINE is not something high
above us. It is in heaven, it is in earth,
it is inside us.

Unite yourself to the cosmos, and the thought of transcendence will disappear. Transcendence belongs to the profane world. When all trace of transcendence vanishes, the true person—the Divine Being—is manifest. Empty yourself and let the Divine function.

You cannot see or touch the Divine with your gross senses. The Divine is within you, not somewhere else. Unite yourself to the Divine, and you will be able to perceive gods wherever you are, but do not try to grasp or cling to them.

THE DIVINE does not like to be shut up in a building. The Divine likes to be out in the open. It is right here in this very body. Each one of us is a miniature universe, a living shrine.

WHEN you bow deeply to the universe, it bows back; when you call out the name of God, it echoes inside you.

THE ART OF PEACE is the religion that is not a religion; it perfects and completes all religions.

THE PATH is exceedingly vast. From ancient times to the present day, even the greatest sages were unable to perceive and comprehend the entire truth; the explanation and teachings of masters and saints express only part of the whole. It is not possible for anyone to speak of such things in their entirety. Just head for the light and heat, learn from the gods, and through the virtue of devoted practice of the Art of Peace, become one with the Divine.

LIBRARY OF CONGRESS
CATALOGING-IN-PUBLICATION DATA

Ueshiba, Morihei.
The art of peace: teachings of
the founder of Aikido/Morihei Ueshiba.
p.   cm.—(Shambhala pocket classics)
ISBN 978-0-87773-851-0 (pbk.)
1. Ueshiba, Morihei—Teachings.
2. Aikido—Philosophy.   3. Conflict
management.   I. Title.   II. Series.
GV1114.35.U39   1992   92-50118
796.8'154—dc20   CIP

SHAMBHALA POCKET CLASSICS

THE ART OF WAR by Sun Tzu
Translated by Thomas Cleary

DHAMMAPADA:
The Sayings of the Buddha
Rendered by Thomas Byrom

HAGAKURE:
The Book of the Samurai
by Yamamoto Tsunetomo
Translated by William Scott Wilson

I CHING:
The Book of Change
Translated by Thomas Cleary

THE MAN WHO PLANTED TREES
by Jean Giono

MINDFULNESS ON THE GO:
Simple Meditation Practices You Can Do Anywhere
by Jan Chozen Bays

(Continued on next page)

THE POCKET CHÖGYAM TRUNGPA
Compiled and edited by Carolyn Gimian

THE POCKET DALAI LAMA
Edited by Mary Craig

THE POCKET EMILY DICKINSON
Edited by Brenda Hillman

THE POCKET HAIKU
Compiled and translated by Sam Hamill

THE POCKET KEN WILBER
Edited by Colin Bigelow

THE POCKET PEMA CHÖDRÖN
Edited by Eden Steinberg

THE POCKET RUMI
Edited by Kabir Helminski

THE POCKET THICH NHAT HANH
Compiled and edited by Melvin McLeod

For a complete list, please visit
www.shambhala.com.